EXTREME CAREERS™

SUBMARINERS

Life in Submarines

Brian Wingate

rosen central™

The Rosen Publishing Group, Inc., New York

To Johnny Tharpe

Published in 2004 by The Rosen Publishing Group, Inc.
29 East 21st Street, New York, NY 10010

Copyright © 2004 by The Rosen Publishing Group, Inc.

First Edition

Library of Congress Cataloging-in-Publication Data

Wingate, Brian.
Submariners : life in submarines / by Brian Wingate.— 1st ed.
    p. cm. — (Extreme careers)
Summary: Examines the careers available to scientists, military, and civilian personnel working on submarines, discussing the necessary education, training, and on-the-job duties.
Includes bibliographical references and index.
ISBN 0-8239-3967-7 (library binding)
1. United States. Navy—Submarine forces—Juvenile literature.
2. United States. Navy—Submarine forces—Vocational guidance—Juvenile literature. [1. United States. Navy—Submarine forces—Vocational guidance. 2. Vocational guidance. 3. Submarines (Ships)] I. Title. II. Series.
V858.W553 2004
359.9'3'0973—dc21

                  2002153688

Manufactured in the United States of America

Contents

Introduction

About 75 percent of Earth's surface is covered with water. But much of the ocean remains a mystery to the people on land. Very few people travel in the mysterious depths of the sea.

The ocean has attracted human beings for centuries, and many have dreamed of living underwater all the time. Today, with more than six billion people on land, the idea of living peacefully under the waves may sound better every day. Jules Verne had that dream when he wrote the classic novel *20,000 Leagues Under the Sea*. Movies like Disney's *The Little Mermaid* and *Atlantis* tell stories of whole civilizations living on the ocean bed, complete with kings and castles and talking crabs.

Books and movies have helped us imagine
life in the ocean. At left, a drawing from
Jules Verne's *20,000 Leagues Under the
Sea*. Above is a still from Disney's animated
film *Atlantis*.

These stories may be fantasies, but some people in
today's world spend most of their working lives
underwater. They are called submariners. "Sub"
means under or below, and "marine" means ocean.
Thus, submariners are people who live and work
underwater. It is a world with dangers that is also
filled with beauty. In the submariner's world, what
happens on land can seem like a faraway dream. If

you are looking for an extreme career, the underwater world may be the perfect fit.

Most submariners spend their time on submarines, but some other options are available. You'll read about an underwater laboratory where scientists live sixty feet below the waves. You'll also learn about the growing business of tourist submarines that ferry vacationers underwater in exotic locations. These are fascinating careers. And businesses are always looking for recruits. Why not you?

Water,
Water
Everywhere

Millions of people make their living from the ocean, as people have for thousands of years. Some fish, some sail, and today many study the water and marine life. Researchers use advanced sonar (a method of using sound waves to locate underwater objects) equipment to hunt for shipwrecks and even buried treasure. They also send down unmanned submersible vehicles to study and record the contents of the sandy bottom of the ocean. These researchers control the submersibles from their boats, which stay on the surface. Scuba divers can stay underwater for several hours with the aid of their oxygen tanks, but they soon have to resurface.

Living Underwater

Of all the people who depend on the ocean for their livelihood, only a select few actually live and work underwater. The deeper waters of the ocean are beautiful and inviting, but they can be unforgiving. The water that supports so much life is not as kind to the human body. That's mostly because of water pressure. As you go deeper in the water, the pressure against your body gets greater and greater. Even at 47 feet (14.3 meters) below the water, the pressure is two and a half times greater than the atmosphere at sea level. If you go too deep, you may not come back up.

If you want to live underwater, you must first protect yourself from water pressure. Then you must create most of the conditions that you are accustomed to having on land. You need air to breathe, water to drink, and food to eat. There is one way to achieve this—on a submarine.

Put simply, submarines are big metal tubes filled with air. Two layers make up the outside body, or hull, of the ship. The outer metal layer makes contact with the water. The inner layer provides extra

Constructing a submarine can take up to five years. Here, the inner and outer hulls are assembled in Groton, Connecticut. Hundreds of people work on a single submarine's construction.

protection against water pressure or collision. The metal hulls can withstand the pressure of the surrounding ocean water, so submarines are able to dive much deeper than any human diver can.

Within that metal shell is a very complex world full of the latest technology. You can think of submarines as the space shuttles of the ocean. Both vehicles are built to undergo tremendous stress and pressure to reach places that no human has ever gone before. However,

Dangers of the Deep

Every career has its risks, and the life of a submariner is no exception. The crushing pressure of the deep ocean has claimed several of the U.S. Navy's finest submarines (and submariners). If something goes wrong and the sub begins to sink, all hope is not lost. After the loss of the *Thresher* and the *Scorpion* in the 1960s, researchers developed a vehicle that could rescue the crew of a sinking sub. A deep submergence rescue vehicle (DSRV) can be flown by airplane to the site where a sub has sunk. The DSRV plunges into the water and locates the sub. It attaches to the submarine's escape hatch and removes twenty-two people at a time to the surface. The DSRV can rescue crews as deep as

If an emergency prevents a submarine from surfacing, a DSRV can be taken to the submarine's location quickly to help submariners escape.

6,000 feet (1823 meters). That's almost 3 miles (4.8 kilometers) down!

even subs are not invincible. Every submarine has a crush depth. Submerging below the crush depth causes the submarine's frame to collapse from the extreme water pressure. Early submarines had a crush depth of only 500 feet or so. Today's high-tech attack subs can go down farther than 1,500 feet without imploding. Their actual crush depth is not known, though any crush depth is said to be 20 to 30 percent greater than the depths at which the sub was tested.

Navy Blue Waters

If you have always wanted to live and work underwater, chances are that you will end up working on a submarine. Subs are simply the only safe way to navigate the deep waters of the ocean.

The U.S. Navy owns and operates many of the submarines in the world today. The year 2000 marked the hundred-year anniversary of submarines in the U.S. Navy. Subs first started cruising the seas in 1900, and they soon turned the tide in the military battles of the twentieth century. Submarines played a large role for the Allied forces in winning World War II (1939–1945).

Over the years, the U.S. Navy has developed subs that are more advanced than anyone had thought possible. Submarines have gone through many stages of development—both successful and unsuccessful— to get them just right. Early submarines were small and cramped, holding fewer than twenty people. These early models spent more time on the surface than they did underwater! Diesel engines, which were smoky and created stinky fumes, powered the navy's first large subs. The engine couldn't run when it was below the water because it needed oxygen to operate. So the sub would sit on the surface while the engine charged up huge battery packs. These battery packs gave the sub its underwater power. When the subs did dive below water, the batteries lasted only an hour. Then the crew had to resurface and recharge the batteries. These were hardly able fighting ships. Crews on a diesel sub smelled like fumes when they came to port. After a short time, the smell soaked into their hair, skin, and clothes. You could smell them coming.

Sub History

When do you think the first submarine was invented? 1900? 1850? It seems that such an amazing invention would be a recent discovery. But, in fact, Cornelius Drebbel built the first functioning submarine in the 1620s. It didn't compare to the subs of today; it was covered in leather and could dive only about 15 feet (4.6 meters) below the surface. It was big enough for one person to fit inside, and the submariner moved it by using oars that stuck out of the sides. This first sub acted like an underwater rowboat.

This early illustration of an underwater ship shows that inventors were dreaming of underwater travel long before it was technologically possible.

This naval submarine is in dock for regular maintenance. Hundreds of submarines are traveling beneath the ocean waters at any given time.

Modern Submarines

Modern subs have eliminated the need for diesel engines. Nuclear generators power most of today's subs. A small nuclear reactor provides all the energy that is needed for the ship's electrical and engine power. More important for the navy, nuclear-powered submarines can stay underwater for many months without resurfacing.

The U.S. Navy has two types of subs: attack submarines and fleet ballistic missile submarines. An attack sub is about 360 feet (109.7 meters) long and 34 feet (10.4 meters) wide. A ballistic missile submarine is about 550 feet (167.6 meters) long and 42 feet (12.8 meters) wide. Nearly 135 people live on each of these subs. The subs have enough room for a cafeteria, sleeping quarters, a nuclear reactor room, a radar room, a movie area, hallways, a kitchen, missile bays, bathrooms, and more. Can you imagine fitting all that into your house?

Submarines plowing through the water look like great beasts of the sea. Because naval personnel spend long months underwater, navy subs have many amenities.

Life Underwater

Living on a sub is a bit like being a human sardine: You are crammed very tightly into a metal container with many other people. It's hard to walk down the hallway without brushing someone's shoulder. If you like big open spaces and get annoyed when someone bumps into you on the bus, submarine life will be a little too close for comfort for you.

Sardine Machine

A submarine may be almost as long as three football fields, but most of that space is filled with equipment and machinery. A navy sub's bow (front) holds its weapons systems. The stern (rear) and sides of the sub are crammed full with engineering equipment and the nuclear reactor. This leaves the middle of the ship for living quarters.

Johnny Tharpe served for eleven months on the U.S.S. *Los Angeles* in the U.S. Navy. The *Los Angeles* is a fast-attack submarine. Tharpe agreed to share his experiences with us throughout this book. He says that the sleeping situation on the sub was not always the most comfortable.

"The living quarters were just a sleeping area. There are three berthing [sleeping] areas that are three bunks high. Under your mattress you have your bunk [storage space] where you can put your personal items and stuff for the deployment. Basically you have enough room in there for your uniforms, some private books or music, and your personal hygiene paraphernalia. That's about all you have. We shared bunks, so when you were on duty, someone else was sleeping in your bunk. That way, you are conserving space. So when you lift up the mattress to get into your personal belongings, it's split in half so that there's one part for you and

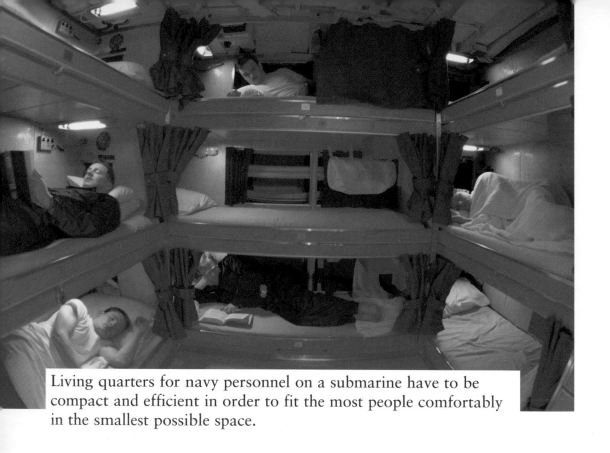

Living quarters for navy personnel on a submarine have to be compact and efficient in order to fit the most people comfortably in the smallest possible space.

another part for whoever is sleeping there the other half of the time."

If you like to jump out of bed in the morning, don't even think about it on a sub. Such an act might give you a splitting headache. On many subs about 18 inches (45.54 centimeters) stand between the top of your mattress and the bunk above you. That means you have just enough space to roll over, but sitting up is out of the question.

The Sub Under Power

If you have a weak stomach, going out on the ocean on a regular boat is a predictable experience. You're out on the waves for a little while, everything looks nice until suddenly—whoomph. Your stomach starts to feel funny and you feel weak in the knees. Seasickness has struck.

The good news for submariners is that there is no seasickness on a submarine. Subs are very stable when they're underwater. The crew controls the depth of the sub by manipulating the amount of air in the sub's ballast tanks. Ballast tanks can hold either air or water. They are located just inside the hull of the ship. A second, thicker hull keeps the water in the ballast tanks from leaking into the ship. If you need to sink, add water to the ballast tanks. If you need to rise, add air. When you add air to the ballast tanks, the sub becomes lighter than the surrounding water and immediately begins to rise. By using the ballast tanks wisely, the crew can keep the sub stable in the water.

Johnny Tharpe described the only way to feel seasick on a sub: "The only time that you feel true seasickness is when they blow all the ballast at one time and do an emergency surface. Even roller-coaster rides at amusement parks have nothing on that. You are literally shooting up like a bullet hundreds of feet below the water, and as you hit the surface, the submarine will shoot 30 to 50 feet (9.1 to 15.2 meters) out of the water and then land. It doesn't happen that often, but that's the only time that you would feel any nausea."

Air and Water Below the Surface

You've probably held your breath and plunged underwater. It doesn't take long before you jump to the surface, gasping for fresh air. But a sub can go under for months and months with more than one hundred people on board who need fresh air to breathe all the time. Do they bring oxygen tanks? No, that would fill half the ship. The answer is pretty amazing. While at sea, the crew uses technology in the submarine to actually make new fresh air and water. What do they start with? Ocean water, of course. A machine called an oxygen generator separates oxygen molecules from distilled seawater and then pumps the oxygen through the ship's air ducts. Another gadget boils seawater

All the conveniences of home are provided on a submarine. Fresh water for drinking, bathing, and shaving is extracted from seawater using a special desalination machine.

until the salt and impurities are separated from the pure water. The result is delicious distilled water. Johnny Tharpe says, "It's as pure as you can get. It's even purer than spring water."

No Windows

Sub life is not like the commercials for cruise ships that you see on television. Subs in the navy don't

On some subs, exercise like jogging can be one way to spend free time.

have portholes. You cannot see all the fish as you pass over coral reefs. Submariners get used to not seeing the outside world, even though they'd see just water. To make sure that submariners can accept being underwater for months, all recruits undergo psychological testing to make sure their temperament matches the life of a submariner.

Great Food

You may have heard that food in the military is awful. You hear tales of people squirting food out of tubes and eating stuff that your dog would refuse. That may be true in other branches of the military, but on a submarine you eat well. Food is always available, and it's always good. Johnny Tharpe told us: "Of all the services, the navy has the best food. You ask anyone who has served in the military, and they'll tell you the same thing. It's a naval tradition going back hundreds of years. And psychologically there's a good reason for it. In the navy you're out to sea and you don't see anything, sometimes for months. So the only perk you have is the food. It's like having comfort food twenty-four hours a day." Crews will sometimes go underwater for months at a time. Tharpe once went down for four months before seeing the sky again.

Jobs on a Submarine

When you are 200 hundred feet (61 meters) below the ocean surface in a cramped space, it suddenly becomes very important for each person to do his job and do it well.

What are the jobs on a typical submarine? If this is your choice for an extreme career, take a look at some of your options. The following jobs are those assigned to submariners on a Trident sub, which is a fleet ballistic missile submarine.

Electrician's Mate (EM)

The electrician's mate monitors all the electrical systems in the ship. Johnny Tharpe describes his job as an electrician's mate: "I'm certified as an electrician, so I handled everything on the sub or everything in the navy that dealt with electricity. That's high voltage, low voltage, or any electrical equipment such as washers, dryers, switchboards, and so on. I also monitored the electrical aspects of the nuclear reactor that ran the ships. In the simplest terms, I would make sure that the nuclear reactor did not explode, and I would monitor the electricity that the reactor produced to run the ship."

Electronics Technician (ET)

Subs are bristling with the latest technologies, and it is the responsibility of electronics technicians to keep things running smoothly. Several different specialties exist within the ET rating. Some ETs operate the nuclear power plant. Others maintain the navigation equipment. Some oversee the entire communication system aboard the sub, which includes computers, sonar, radar, and other navigational data.

Fire Control Technician (FT)

A fire control technician takes care of the sub's weapons control systems. In the U.S. Navy, subs are used as floating weapons depots. Every naval sub carries a mind-boggling amount of advanced weaponry. This fact helps convince other countries that it would be unwise to go to war against the United States. With all that firepower on board, FTs make sure that everything is in tip-top shape and ready to respond to any emergency.

Helmsman

While everyone stays busy in the back of the sub, someone has to keep his eyes on the road—er, the sea. The helmsman sits at the helm and steers the ship. In a navy sub, the helmsman may be as young as eighteen years old. Every new submariner trains extensively at submarine school before taking the wheel of a brand new $750 million vehicle. We'll get a glimpse of sub school in chapter 5.

These fire control technicians monitor the various weapon systems on board a naval submarine. They coordinate their work with that of the sonar techs and missile techs.

Hospital Corpsman (HM)

When you become ill at the bottom of the ocean, you can't phone your family doctor for an appointment. The hospital corpsman is the ship's medical doctor. He treats all medical problems the crew encounters. The HM also makes sure that conditions are healthy on board. The hospital corpsman examines the air and water systems and also food preparation so that everything is sanitary. Since everyone eats the same food, one batch of food poisoning could affect the entire crew and jeopardize a mission.

Machinist Mate (MM)

This is a dream job for people who love motors and mechanical systems of all kinds. The MMs operate and repair all of the mechanical systems. These include everything from the blender in the kitchen to the nuclear reactor and the sub's propulsion system.

Mess Management Specialist (MS)

A mess management specialist sounds like a housekeeper who cleans up after everyone on the ship. In the armed services, however, a meal is called a mess. The MS makes sure that everyone eats well. This job is not simple with so many people on board. Subs can carry enough food for a ninety-day mission. The mess management specialist has to plan how much food to bring aboard. Once at sea, it's too late to stop at the supermarket. After that ninety days, the sub meets with another ship on the ocean to replenish food, stores, and any other needed equipment for another ninety-day period.

Missile tubes open and close at the flip of a switch. Part of a crew's mission is making sure that sensitive military hardware is always in proper working order.

Missile Technician (MT)

When you've got missiles on board your sub, it's good to know that someone's taking care of them. That's the job of the MTs. They repair and prepare the missiles for action and operate the sub's weapons control system. Submarines can fire missiles from an underwater location and strike a target on land that is hundreds of miles away. Compressed air shoots the missiles from the ship, through the water, and into the air above. Then a fueled rocket ignites and the missile shoots off toward its target.

Store Keeper (SK)

With all the repairs going on, where do the replacement parts come from? The store keeper is in charge of replacement parts on board. Before each mission the SK prepares for every imaginable situation. Multiple replacement parts for every machine are available in case of failure. If a part becomes unavailable, the SK

Sonar techs are always listening for sounds of ships on or below the water. They plot ship positions on electronic boards so that they always know who is out there.

orders another for shipment during the next stores replenishing stop (often somewhere far out at sea).

Sonar Technician (ST)

Without the sonar technician, a submarine would be blind in the water. Sonar techs know how to decode the sounds that come back to the sub from the sonar

Cross-training

When a submarine is hundreds of yards below the ocean's surface, even a small accident can grow into an emergency situation that threatens the lives of the entire crew. If you are on a sub crew, you must be ready for anything. That is the main reason why many crew members are cross-trained in their duties. Athletes who cross-train participate in many different sports: They run, then they swim, and then maybe they do some yoga. Cross-training helps keep your body in top shape, and it also helps you avoid injuries. Cross-training on a submarine works the same way. When you begin to learn your specific job on the ship, you will also learn how to do other people's jobs.

Johnny Tharpe explains how he was cross-trained for his job as electrician's mate: "I learned how the water system cools the reactor, how pipes are flowing, the hydraulics of the cooling system, and the hydraulics of the nuclear rods. I also studied the more computerized end of things. Even though I was an electrician's mate, I could also do the ET [electronic technician] jobs and the MT [mechanical technician] jobs."

system. The word "sonar" stands for "sound navigation and ranging." Like bats or dolphins, subs make their way underwater by hearing the world around them. Today's subs have active and passive sonar systems. Active sonar sends out sound waves that make a pinging sound when they bounce off the metal surface of other ships. The passive sonar system just listens closely to the surrounding waters without sending out sound waves. Trained sonar technicians learn to recognize all the different sounds of the ocean. Through sonar frequencies, they can recognize other ships, schools of fish, and even approaching icebergs.

Torpedoman's Mate (TM)

The TM is responsible for all the torpedo tubes on board. If torpedoes are being fired during a training exercise or in combat, the TM supervises the crew as it reloads the tubes. Torpedoes were the first weapons on submarines to make a major impact in battle. When fired from the front of the sub, they streak through the water at their targets. Torpedoes can carry either TNT-type explosive devices or nuclear bombs.

Yeoman (YN)

With everyone working on engines, sonar, and missiles, somebody has to do the paperwork. The yeoman is the person who files paperwork and supervises the communications that are received from other ships.

Other Sub Jobs

Many other "jobs" pop up in the underwater city of a submarine. Somebody has to be the barber, and someone has to clean up after dinner. These extra jobs are divided among the crew. Every sailor finishing a work shift has specific cleanup duties that keep the sub running smoothly.

Other Underwater Adventures

4

Some 3 miles (4.8 kilometers) off the coast of Florida, scientists are hard at work in a laboratory under the waves. This lab, called *Aquarius*, is 62 feet (18.9 meters) below the surface. *Aquarius* is nestled among the coral reefs in Florida Keys National Marine Sanctuary. This protected area is home to countless species of fish and other water creatures. The researchers and scientists on board have the perfect place to study the life that swims around them. The *Aquarius* scientists don't miss the perks of home while they're underwater: They have all the latest equipment and technology, including Internet access. The National Oceanic and Atmospheric Administration (NOAA) owns the lab. Unlike naval subs, *Aquarius* welcomes female scientists aboard.

The lab *Aquarius* gives scientists the opportunity to conduct underwater research and experiments. Like all submarines, there is little room because space is used for scientific equipment.

Life on *Aquarius*

What the scientists on *Aquarius* do miss is space! Submarines are pretty small, and *Aquarius* is actually much smaller than a submarine. The lab and living area is 9 feet (2.7 meters) wide and 43 feet (13.1 meters) long. The crew has about 400 square feet of space in which to live and work. That's only the size of a single room that is 20 feet

(6.1 meters) long and 20 feet wide. No more than six people can work in *Aquarius* at the same time.

Unlike a nuclear sub that may stay underwater for months, crews can work in the *Aquarius* for up to ten days at a time. They have found that these ten-day missions are as productive as most sixty-day missions on the surface. Why? It can be very hard to conduct research from a boat at the surface of the ocean when you are at the mercy of the weather and the waves. If a big storm rolls in, you must pack up your equipment and head home. Subs are unaffected by even the heaviest storms on the surface.

Diving from Underwater Homes

Another big advantage for the *Aquarius* is something called saturation diving. When divers are able to live 62 feet (18.9 meters) under the surface of the waves, their bodies get used to the different concentrations of gases and pressure at that depth. The pressure of the atmosphere in *Aquarius* is about 2.5 times greater than at sea level. So when they do their diving missions into the surrounding waters, they can stay at

Underwater Science

Since the late 1990s, scientists have made some great discoveries while working on *Aquarius*. Here are some of the things that they have studied.

• Scientists documented that ultraviolet radiation from the sun is damaging coral reef environments. This is occurring at a greater rate now because of the growing hole in the ozone layer.

• It gets pretty dark in the ocean, and as you get deeper, light becomes very important. *Aquarius* scientists are studying how fish use light and color to communicate with each other. From these scientific studies, we can learn more about the workings of color vision and night vision.

• The fossil record has taught us much about life on Earth, from dinosaurs to early hominids. The ocean also contains many fossils that have been buried or undiscovered for thousands of years. *Aquarius* divers are studying the fossils in the coral reefs and learning more about what happened to the ocean over the years.

the bottom for as long as they want—or until they need to refill their oxygen tanks! Other divers who descend from the surface can stay at the bottom for only about eighty minutes before they begin to get sick from the pressure.

Time-share Laboratory

Aquarius is not home to one single crew or team of researchers. Many different groups use the lab throughout the year. They share the facility by taking turns for each ten-day mission. The National Aeronautics and Space Administration (NASA) trains astronauts at *Aquarius* because many of the conditions are similar to weightlessness in space.

Before moving in for a mission, scientists must first train for underwater living. Every incoming crew must train for five days before the ten-day mission.

Tourist Subs

Not all submarines are used by the military and scientists. You've probably noticed the shimmering blue

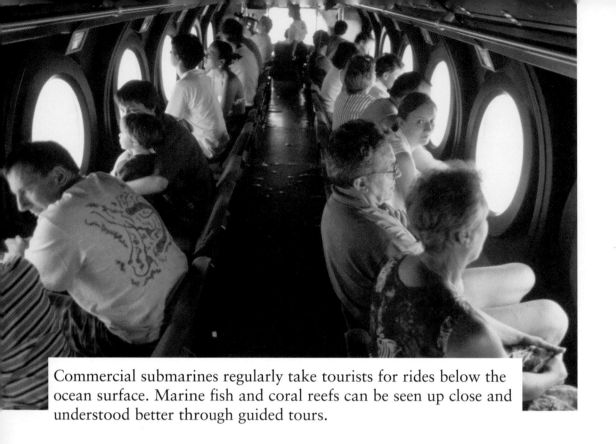

Commercial submarines regularly take tourists for rides below the ocean surface. Marine fish and coral reefs can be seen up close and understood better through guided tours.

waters, the coral reefs, and the colorful fish in photos you have seen of Hawaii, Bermuda, Florida, and other such places. Wouldn't it be cool to explore those waters every day when you went to work? And what if other people would pay you to take them on a tour of the ocean floor? That is what some people do for a living. All it takes is a tourist submarine and a great location on the coast with plenty of travelers passing through.

In some areas of the world, tourist submarines are growing in popularity. Some two million passengers ride on tourist subs each year. In most areas, tourists pay about $100 for a fifty-minute ride. Passengers sit in the middle of the sub and face the sides, where large viewing ports allow them to see the ocean world as they pass through the water.

Tourist subs differ greatly from navy submarines because they don't have to lug around all that equipment around the ocean. Next to a navy sub, tourist subs look like little babies alongside a mother whale. Without the weight of equipment and weapons, nuclear power isn't necessary—these subs run on very powerful batteries.

As you might expect, it takes a lot of money to buy your own submarine. But who said you have to own your own sub anyway? With a little effort you can join the crew of one of the subs already operating today. Most tourist subs have a staff of about thirty-five people who handle all of the aspects of the business. Some people sell tickets while others handle the maintenance of the sub's equipment. Hopefully you will be the one steering the sub. If you are, you will get more time underwater than you thought was possible. You'll give about eleven rides per day, with each ride lasting fifty minutes. So that's ten hours a day underwater!

Scientists Under Ice

You don't have to be in the U.S. Navy to spend time on one of its nuclear subs. Scientists often take trips on navy subs for special research trips that can only be done underwater. A navy sub is the perfect vehicle for a research trip to a dangerous place like the North Pole.

Traveling by water to the North Pole has always been dangerous because of the huge icebergs that can puncture and sink any ship. Even if you can get around the icebergs, you eventually reach the polar ice caps. At that point, solid ice stretches as far as the eye can see. Ships cannot go farther.

Subs have a way of avoiding icebergs and the polar ice caps: They go under them. Today's submarines routinely go beneath the ice caps at Earth's opposite poles. Their sonar equipment warns them if they are approaching any ice, and they can then change course. This makes submarines a great research vehicle for scientists at the North Pole.

The U.S.S. *Nautilus* was the world's first nuclear submarine, and it amazed the world in August 1958

The first nuclear-powered submarine, the U.S.S. *Nautilus*, was launched in January 1954. It routinely prowled the waters below the North Pole's ice cap.

when it cruised right under the polar ice cap to the North Pole. The navy has continued this tradition today by building twenty-three new subs that have special under-ice capabilities. Their diving planes retract into the hull to prevent any damage from ice. In June 2001, the navy sub U.S.S. *Scranton* became the first of these redesigned subs to surface at the North Pole.

Getting There from Here

5

The world's a big place, and the ocean makes up most of it. If your dream is to make your home under the waves with the fish and the whales, it can happen. Now that you have a glimpse of the underwater life, it's time to plot your course for the future. The options for those who want to live the life of a submariner are wide and varied. The future, with society's eye on ever-increasing technology, will without doubt increase the opportunities for humans' quest to live underwater.

Sea Cadets

For some people, the call of the ocean is something that they feel in their bones from an early age. As

The Navy League Cadet Corps offers young people a look at naval life. The corps teaches strength of mind and body and a strong work ethic that cadets carry with them throughout their lives.

early as elementary school, they just know that the submarine life is for them. The earliest age for U.S. Navy enlistment is eighteen years old. If you really want to get a taste of the navy life, however, you don't have to wait that long.

The navy offers two training programs that are open to young men and women ages eleven to seventeen. The Navy League Cadet Corps is for ages eleven to thirteen. The Naval Sea Cadet Corps accepts teens from thirteen to seventeen. These programs are a good way to see if military life is for you. Both programs offer training in nautical practices, water safety, swimming, and other skills such as tying knots and splicing. Cadets also learn military drills and history. The Naval Sea Cadet Corps even participates in a two-week boot camp that is a smaller version of the navy's own boot camp. Once that is completed, you get to the fun part: cruising in a submarine!

If you graduate from the Sea Cadets program and decide to enlist in the navy, you enter at a higher rank than other recruits. Not a bad deal! You can find out more about these programs at www.seacadets.org.

Before You Dive

You are standing in a room that is rapidly filling with water. A pipe in front of you is gushing water, and it seems that you can do nothing to stop it. Several of your classmates try to stop the leak, but the water keeps coming. Alarms screech in your ears. Your heart pounds. You fight thoughts of disaster, drowning, death! Welcome to sub school.

In sub school, students are forced to react quickly and work as a team. Almost every possible disaster is practiced so that submariners are prepared for the unexpected.

All recruits learn fire-fighting techniques. Working together during such a crisis can mean the difference between life and death for submariners.

If you join the U.S. Navy for submarine duty, you will undergo extensive training even before you set foot on a submarine. Every candidate for submarine duty must graduate from sub school, otherwise known as SUBSCOL. At sub school, you are put through the paces of anything and everything that can happen on a sub. After the five-week training, you may think that your middle name is submarine. You learn about submarine maintenance, navigation, and weapons systems. You also learn about

A submarine simulator re-creates emergencies that help recruits train thoroughly for unexpected situations.

communications, administration, and naval tactics.

SUBSCOL is no ordinary classroom environment. It is a state-of-the-art, knock-your-socks-off, full-throttle experience. The submarine school is actually a huge campus of buildings located in Groton, Connecticut. The navy has spared no expense in creating an environment that is perfect for learning the basics of working and living on a submarine.

Simulator rooms that re-create submarine conditions are located throughout the school. This is where you'll learn to deal with possible emergencies. Some rooms have raging fires that you must extinguish. Other rooms have bursting pipes that rapidly fill the room with water. You and the other students must learn to solve the problem before the simulator "sinks." All of the simulations are supervised so nobody gets hurt, but the fear of these situations is very real. By the time you step on board a real sub, you will be ready to handle any challenge that comes your way.

You may also receive additional training if you have a specialized job on the ship. Johnny Tharpe describes the training he received as a nuclear electrician's mate: "We went down to what they call nuclear power school, which requires six and a half months of training in school after boot camp. We learned about nuclear reactors and fusion reactors, along with basic principles of nuclear physics. It also included learning how to qualify to be an electrician's mate, which is basically getting certified as an electrician—the same kind of electrician that comes to your home to fix the electrical wiring in your house."

Women and Subs—The United States and Canada

Someday, Karen O'Connell may be seen as a hero for any Canadian woman who wants to be a submariner.

Subs of the Future

What will submarines look like when it's your turn to take the helm? Within the U.S. Navy, a group is working hard to create the submarine of the future. The Submarine Future Studies Group wants the navy to stay on the cutting edge of technology to maintain its superiority in the military fleet. Some of its ideas include:

• Launching unmanned aerial vehicles from submerged submarines. These remote-controlled craft (similar to a remote-controlled model plane) can spy on surrounding territory and send back valuable target information. These will be very small to avoid detection, some as small as 3 inches (7.6 centimeters) wide.

• Creating docking bays on subs that can receive under-water vehicles. This would enable the crew to receive supplies while still underwater.

• Developing an aerosub that will sneak up to an enemy shore underwater and then fly like an aircraft, zooming over land to strike enemy targets.

Source: *Sea Power*, July 2001

On March 8, 2001, the Canadian government authorized women to serve on Canada's subs. Not long afterward, Canadian Navy lieutenant Karen Elizabeth O'Connell was the first woman to be accepted for submarine duty.

Women wanting to serve on a U.S. Navy submarine will have to wait a while longer. The U.S. Navy does not allow women to serve on sub crews. The navy believes that the lack of space and privacy make it impossible for both sexes to work together comfortably. Many groups are pressuring the navy to accept women on subs, and some promising signs indicate that the situation may change in the future.

People of the Sea

The underwater life is one that offers many dangers and rewards. People who have served on a submarine or an underwater research vessel never feel the same again. They say the experience changes you for the better. They have explored a world that few people ever see. They also bring back stories and information that help the world understand the mysterious ocean.

Maybe you'll buy a tourist sub and be the best tour guide in the whole ocean. Perhaps the navy is for you. Researching underwater life or studying humans living underwater are both wide-open fields. Living in such a small space with other people creates a bond and a sense of community that will last the rest of your life. Many sub crews are still in touch by phone and over the Internet. When you choose to live and work underwater, you are not just gaining a career. You are gaining a family.

Glossary

ballast Heavy material that is placed in the hold of a ship to enhance stability.

ballistic A term relating to the motion of objects moving under their own momentum and the force of gravity.

deployment The distribution of personnel and equipment for a military mission.

distill To separate or extract the essential elements of something.

hominid The family of living things that consists of human beings and their early humanlike ancestors.

hull The frame or body of a ship.

missile An object or weapon that is fired, thrown, dropped, or otherwise projected at a target.

sonar A system using transmitted and reflected underwater sound waves to detect and locate submerged objects or measure the distance to the floor of a body of water.

submersible A vessel capable of operating or remaining underwater.

torpedo A cigar-shaped, self-propelled underwater projectile launched from a submarine and designed to explode on contact with a target.

For More Information

Organizations

Canadian Navy
Department of National Defense
Major-General George R. Pearkes Building
101 Colonel By Drive
Ottawa, ON K1A OK2
(613) 995-2434
Web site: http://www.navy.dnd.ca

Naval Submarine League
P.O. Box 1146
5025-D Backlick Road
Annandale, VA 22003
(703) 256-8891
Web site: http://www.navalsubleague.com

Submariners: Life in Submarines

The Naval Submarine League has a directory of all the former navy subs that now rest in museums throughout the United States.

Navy League Cadet Corps
2300 Wilson Boulevard
Arlington, VA 22201
(703) 243-6910
Web site: http://www.seacadets.org

Web Sites

Due to the changing nature of Internet links, the Rosen Publishing Group, Inc., has developed an online list of Web sites related to the subject of this book. This site is updated regularly. Please use this link to access the list:

http://www.rosenlinks.com/ec/subm

For Further Reading

Clancy, Tom. *Submarine: A Guided Tour Inside a Nuclear Warship*. New York: Berkeley Publishing Group, 1993.

Graham, Ian S. *Boats, Ships, Submarines and Other Floating Things (How Things Work)*. New York: Kingfisher Books, 1993.

Jefferis, David. *Read About Submarines*. New York: Warwick Press, 1990.

Jefferis, David. *Super Subs: Exploring the Deep Sea*. New York: Crabtree Publishing, 2002.

Payan, Gregory. *Life on a Submarine*. Danbury, CT: Children's Press, 2000.

Weiss, Harvey. *Submarines and Other Underwater Craft*. New York: Thomas Y. Crowell, 1990.

Bibliography

Benson, Robert. "Rising Water Level." *All Hands*, April 1999. Retrieved August 15, 2002 (http://www.medi-acen.navy.mil/pubs/allhands/apr99/pg18.htm).

Fuentes, Gidget. "Still No Women on Subs." *Navy Times*, November 8, 1999, Vol. 49, No. 5, p. 22.

Jefferis, David. *Read About Submarines*. New York: Warwick Press, 1990.

Jones, L. Bruce. "The Tourist Submarine Industry: A Summary Article." U.S. Submarines, Inc., 1996. Retrieved June 29, 2002 (http://www.ussubs.com/News_folder/article.t-sub.industry.html).

Kreisher, Otto. "Innovations Under the Sea." *Sea Power*, July 2001, Vol. 44, No. 7, p. 42.

Moniz, Walter, and John Burlage. "Sub Merging the Sexes." *Navy Times*, May 13, 2002, Vol. 51, No. 32, p. 4.

"Ship's Crew." Public Affairs Office, Kings Bay Submarine Office. Retrieved August 12, 2002 (http://www.ssbn640.com/blue_gold.htm).

Spotts, Peter N. "What It's Like to Sail Under the Sea." *Christian Science Monitor*, May 25, 1999, Vol. 91, No. 125, p. 22.

"Sub Breaks the Ice." *Navy Times*, June 25, 2001, Vol. 50, No. 38, p. 2.

Tharpe, Johnny. Personal interview conducted by author. August 22, 2002.

Weiss, Harvey. *Submarines and Other Underwater Craft*. New York: Thomas Y. Crowell, 1990.

Index

About the Author

Although Brian Wingate has never actually lived underwater, he has been fond of the ocean. He once spent four months at sea and also toured a Trident nuclear submarine. He is currently land-locked in Tennessee.

Photo Credits

Cover © Greg Mathieson/MAI/Timepix; p. 5 (*Atlantis*) © Reuters/Timepix; pp. 5 (*20,000 Leagues Under the Sea*), 43 © Bettmann/Corbis; pp. 9, 21, 27, 29 © Steve Kaufman/Corbis; pp. 10, 14, 31, 48, 49, 50 © Yogi Inc./Corbis; pp. 13, 15 © Corbis; pp. 18, 22 © Roger Ressmeyer/Corbis; pp. 36, 46 © AP/Wide World Photos; p. 40 © Philip Gould/Corbis.

Designer: Les Kanturek; Editor: Mark Beyer